Contents

Introduction

Did you know that there are 24 species of hamster?

The most common are the Syrian and Dwarf hamsters. Syrian are your regular size hamster, probably around 8 inches long. They go by names such as Teddy Bear hamster, Golden hamster, and so forth.

But, you want to go small, huh? Then the Dwarf hamster is for you! They grow to a maximum length of 4 inches.

There are four species or types

These are:- Campbell's or Djungarians, Roborovskis, Siberians or Winter Whites, and Chinese. Siberians and Campbell's are very closely related, but always remember they are two different species, so you can't mix them.

So, you think owning a Campbells hamster might be kind of fun?

Well, it is! They are social and prefer to live with a cage mate, unlike Syrians, who can't live together.

Campbell's form colonies and families. They raise their pups together and sometimes form strong, bonds with one another.

2

Top Tips

A must have...

→ A cage
→ Wood shavings
→ Bedding
→ Exercise wheel
→ Nest box
→ Water bottle
→ Food bowls
→ Chew sticks
→ Food

Never, ever use cedar shavings!

These cause respiratory problems in dwarf hamsters, so don't even try it!

HAMSTER

The perfect pet?...

Oh yes...they sleep most of the day and wake when the family returns home from school and work.

They are attractive, entertaining, easy to care for and don't smell if their homes are cleaned regularly. This makes them ideal pets for the modern family.

3

Quality time...

Be prepared to put in some quality time with your hamster in order to tame it.

This requires the owner to clean, feed, water and handle the hamster so that it becomes familiar with you. Only then can you enjoy each other's company.

Varieties

4

The most common of the larger varieties are the Golden/Syrian Hamster. They come from the desert areas of the Middle East.

Of the smaller, Dwarf species, Russians are found in central Asia and Siberia and Campbell's live among the sand dunes of Northern Russia and Northern China.

5

Chinese Hamster

Strictly speaking, the Chinese hamster is a member of the Rat-like hamster group. Chinese hamsters are commonly kept and sold as pets in the U.K. They have longer, slimmer bodies than Russian hamsters, with small tails up to 2cm in length. The markings are quite different, with a well defined straight line separating the belly fur from the browner fur over the back and head.

Chinese hamsters are tame, easy to handle and are reported to live a little longer than other hamsters. They prefer sharing accommodation in pairs or trio's rather than large groups.

6

Campbell's Hamster

Often referred to simply as "Campbell's", these are probably the most widely kept and sold variety of Dwarf hamster. They are very sociable and may be kept in pairs or larger groups.

7

Russian Hamster

At first sight, the Winter White looks very similar to its close relative, the Campbell, but the two are distinct species and should not be mated.

There are several colour and coat varieties available in Campbell's hamsters in addition to the normal grey-brown agouti.

Albino

They are true albinos with pure white fur, pink eyes and flesh-coloured ears. Albino is inherited as a simple recessive trait.

Argente

Now with its own "official" standard, Argente is produced by a single recessive gene, and has an orange tint to the coat, with similar markings to the normal grey Campbell.

Wavy/Satin

Both coat types have recently been described, and may be combined with any of the above colour/spotting genes.

8

Golden Hamsters come in a variety of colours, ranging form dark golden to grey and black.

Golden hamsters are best housed alone compared to the Dwarf hamsters, who enjoy being sociable.

9

Roborovskis Hamster

The Roborovski hamster is the baby of the family, and also the speediest. They do not usually bite, but are difficult to handle on account of their size.

They do not appear to have any major differences in either housing or dietary requirements compared to other Dwarf species, although plastic tanks are probably more suitable than wire mesh cages for housing, in view of their small size.

Choosing your Hamster

10

Boy or girl? How can you tell?

This is a frequently asked question that everyone needs to know the answer to. Telling the difference is a little tricky at first, so here's a handy tip:-

To determine the sex, check the distance between the anus and genital opening, which is wider in the male than female.

Adult males have a more pointed bottom than the females.

Of course, the store staff can confirm your hamster's sex for you.

11

Your hamster should have shiny fur, a clean bottom (soiling may mean diarrhoea), bright clear eyes and should breath easily.

The hamsters home should always be clean. A dirty cage means a potentially sick hamster.

Do not be alarmed if you can see a dark patch on each hip of your hamster, it is the sweat gland.

12

When transporting your hamster, you will need a small ventilated carry box. For short journeys, a cardboard box is suitable.

Alternatively, it is worth buying a small plastic container, which can be used as a 'holding pen' when you clean out the cage or for future visits to the vets.

Your Hamster...

As hamsters sleep the majority of the day, they may be asleep when you go to look at them. When gently wakened, the hamster should be curious and not sluggish.

If it remains slow and sluggish, it may be ill.

Housing your Hamster

13

Wire cages

Allow your hamster to use it as a climbing frame. They also provide good ventilation which helps reduce respiratory diseases.

If you choose a wire cage, make sure it has a deep plastic tray base so that the shavings create a good burrowing area for the hamster.

Make sure with the store staff that the wire cage is suited to your hamster as he may be able to get between the wires.

14

Glass or plastic tanks also make good hamster homes, as long as they have a ventilated lid.

They provide great visibility, are cat proof, easy to clean and can accommodate a good depth of shavings for burrowing.

15

Location, location, location

Don't stand the cage in direct sunlight or in a draught.

Choose a peaceful area of the house to put the hamster cage or tank so that he/she will be undisturbed during the daytime.

It is important that the temperature is comfortable.

A cold or unheated room may cause the hamster to hibernate.

Regular cleaning is important to reduce the smell of urine.

Tubes act as climbing frames as well as tunnels, which will help keep your hamster fit and healthy.

Top Tips

Do not buy a wire cage if you have a cat. Their claws can easily hook through the wires and injure your hamster.

Plastic linking systems let your hamsters explore and access different areas and levels of the tank. These linking tube systems are designed to mimic a hamster burrow.

HAMSTER

Food Guide

16

**Did you know hamster means hoarder?
...and hamsters do hoard food.**

To satisfy the hamsters need to hoard food, place more dry food than he needs to eat each day. Limit the amount of perishable food as you don't want the surplus to decay.

Hamsters have large cheek pouches in which they can carry half their body weight in food.

These are not noticeable when empty, but bulge when full.

17

Food glorious food

Dry food such as grains, seeds and nuts are the basis of the hamster diet. Too many peanuts and sunflower seeds in the mix can lead to an obese hamster.

Instead, buy the traditional mixture or pelted food blocks.

18

Fruit & Veg...

Small amounts of fresh fruit and vegetables should be added as a healthy supplement to your hamsters diet.

Do not overdose your hamster on the fresh food as it causes digestive upsets.

One broccoli floret or one slice of apple per day is ample.

19

Include protein

Twice a week provide your hamster with some protein. Try offering a slice of hard boiled egg, a slice of cooked chicken or a teaspoon of cottage cheese.

Play time

Keeping you hamster active

Without exercise he will grow flabby and unhealthy. If you do let your hamster out of his cage, beware of cables and other human hazards.

Remember, they are constant gnawers so keep electrical cables and plants out of reach.

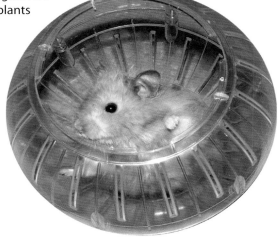

Daily exercise

Keep your hamster active by buying him/her an exercise wheel. Most hamsters love their wheels, but some can become addicted to it and run themselves to exhaustion!

Never let your hamster explore the house unsupervised and keep him/her away from stairs and steps.

HAMSTER

22

Exercise balls

Help protect your hamster and keep him/her fit as he rolls around the house.

Let him roll around for 10 to 20 minutes under supervision.

Grooming

23

And smile...

Hamster's teeth constantly grow and need to be ground down by chewing.

Hard hamster treats or mineral stones help to keep their teeth the right length.

24

Check your hamster's bottom!

It only takes a few minutes to check for a dirty bottom. Hamsters are clean animals, so signs of diarrhoea may mean a digestive upset.

If droppings attach to the fur, wipe them off with a damp sponge, trying not to wet the fur.

25

Clean. Clean. Clean.

Hamster's groom themselves constantly.

If your hamster enjoys gentle stroking, use a soft

toothbrush. This will help remove bits of residual dust that stick to the fur.

If your hamster fur becomes ruffled or dull looking, this is often a first sign of illness.

Scent glands are located on your hamster's hip. The gland patch may be darker, wet or even be bald.

HAMSTER

If you accustom your hamster to this process it will help when he is older and can no longer clean himself properly.

There is no need to bath your hamster unless he falls into something sticky.

Cage Care

26

Home Sweet Home

Keep your hamster home clean with a daily spring clean. Each day remove any wet bedding and clean out the toilet area.

Remove any uneaten food in particular fruit or vegetables. Wash out the food bowl, refill the water bottle and check for leaks and blockages.

27

Safety first

Check your hamster cage for damaged areas.

In a wire cage, look out for rusting and ensure that all catches are secure.

In tanks, inspect sealants for signs of gnawing.

All hamsters are born escapologists and will work at a weak area until they have made an exit hole.

28

A clean house is a happy house

Cages should be cleaned fully every two weeks. Throw out old shavings and scrub out the corners of the cage using a safe detergent from the pet shop.

Nest boxes and bedding inside can usually be left for four weeks or so.

While you are carrying out your daily hamster house keeping, pop your hamster into a holding cage or exercise ball.

Chew sticks or chew toys help to wear down the ever-growing teeth of your hamster. If you don't give them chew sticks, they will chew on something else, like your brand new cage!

HAMSTER

Handling your Hamster

29

Don't rush

When you bring your new hamster home, don't rush to handle him. Allow a few days for him to settle in.

He won't be relaxed until he marks his cage with his own scent.

Let him then get used to your voice and the smell of your fingers. Don't make big awkward movements with your hand, remember how small he is and how big your hand must look. Once he has learned to trust you, try tempting him with a treat. If this works then try to pick him up.

30

Hold me close

If your hamster accepts your presence and allows you to pick him up, cup both hands together and then scoop the hamster up.

Once he gets used to being handled, try picking him up with one hand.

This is done by carefully placing one hand around the hamster's body, with his head pointing towards your wrist.

31

Not too **high..**

Try to be sitting down when you handle your hamster, so that if he does wriggle free he will not hurt himself if he falls.

Top Tips

If he bites, its because he is frightened.

To avoid being bitten follow these guidelines:

→ Don't pick him up when he is asleep.
→ Talk quietly to your hamster so that he becomes aware of your presence.
→ Always wash your hands before and after holding him.
→ Remember to keep movements slow and gentle.

HAMSTER

32

Topsy Turvy

If your hamster throws himself on his back and screams when your hand goes near him, don't panic. He still thinks of you as a predator.

Offer him treats until he knows your smell.

Know your Hamster

Sleep time

33

Hamster's are creatures that come out in the evening and early morning.

A hamster should be allowed to wake up when he chooses.

Once your hamster knows you and your routine, he will be quite happy to emerge in the evenings when he hears you.

34

Brrr...

Hamster's fall into a deep sleep if the temperature drops too low. In this state, your hamster will appear to be dead, don't panic. If you find your hamster stiff and cold during winter, place the cage in a warmer room.

When exposed to the warmer temperature, a hibernating hamster will slowly wake up.

35

Know his behaviour

Squeaking

Your hamster may squeak for attention or if he is agitated.

Clicking

If you can hear a repeated clicking sound, this is an indication that your hamster is happy.

Teeth grinding

Your hamster is annoyed.

This could be because he has been disturbed from his sleep. If you try and pick him up, he may bite you.

CLICK CLICK CLICK!

Breeding Advice

36

Golden rules of breeding

Know why you have chosen to breed this litter.

Make sure you breed only from healthy, well looked after hamsters.

Know what you will do with the babies before they are born.

37

Male versus female

Introduce males and females with caution. Use a separate cage when introducing each hamster. Let each hamster spend time to become accustomed to one another's scent.

Mating between Dwarf hamsters will only occur when the female permits it. Scent plays a vital role in the reproduction of Dwarf hamsters; the male can smell when the female is fertile.

38

Pregnancy

The gestation period is usually 15 to 18 days. During this time make sure the female has extra rations of food.

Never disturb her nest or the babies which can be anything from one to twenty in litter size.

The average litter size is 6.

Top Tips

Baby hamsters are born blind and with no fur.

Fur begins to grow after 7 days.

Some hamster varieties should never be mixed.

Breeding two black eyed whites produces a large proportion without eyes.

Female hamsters reach breeding age at 4-6 weeks, but breeding is not advised at this age as it will stunt the female's growth.

Always wash your hands before and after holding him.

Remember to keep movements slow and gentle.

39

Babies

Baby hamsters grow very quickly, so will need plenty of food.

Do not handle or even touch the babies until their eyes open. As soon as they open their eyes, begin to handle them. This handling at an early age will ensure that they become tame. By 25 to 28 days, the hamsters should be fully weaned and the mother removed.

Following this separation, the hamster babies should be split up into single sex groups.

THE HAMSTER
More Information

NATIONAL HAMSTER COUNCIL CLUBS

The Midland Hamster Club

Secretary - Elaine Skidmore
8, Braithwaite Drive
Kingswinford
DY6 8DS
Tel: 01384 298191

The South of England Hamster Club

Secretary - Sue Carter
24 Shepherds Rise
Vernham Dean
Andover
Hampshire
SP11 0HD
Tel: 01264 73741

The Northern Hamster Club

Secretary - Pat Richardson
7 Main Avenue
Heworth
York
YO3 0RT
Tel: 01904 41342

The Heart of England Club

Secretary - Steve Roach
24 Huntercombe Lane (North)
Taplow
SL6 OLG
Tel: 01628 664874

The Southern Hamster Club

Secretary - Wendy Barry
42 Stonebridge Drive
Frome
Somerset
BA11 2TN
Tel: 01373 300766

The Hamster Society

14 Dawn Close
Ness
South Wirral
L64 4DS

The Northern Ireland Hamster Club

Secretary - Rachel Cooper
4 Rusheyhill Road
Lisburn
Co. Antrim
BT28 3TD
Tel: 028 9264 8133

Clubs Affiliated to The British Hamster Association

PO Box 825
Sheffield
S17 3RU